KINGDOM OF MIND

KINGDOM OF MIND

A TALE TO UNDERSTAND AND MASTER OCD

BY S. K. CLARK

ISBN-13: 978-1541339392
ISBN-10: 1541339398

For Robert

"Piu bella cosa non c'e'
Piu bella cosa di te
Unica come sei
Immensa quando vuoi
Grazie di esistere"

-Eros Ramazzotti

Acknowledgements

Thank you to Nia, my rock, love you forever

Thank you to my own Mr. (Greg) Lane,
who helped me through

Thank you to Lexi, my Star

Thank you to Luca, my
Tech Expert

& Thank you to Cam, my Encourager

Love you for always

It had only been two weeks since Liv's last visit to the middle school principal's office. Having already counted the ceiling tiles, she sat in the waiting room, head in hand, waiting to tell her side of the story.

The voice of the reigning sixth-grade bully still circled in her head. "Or what?" he'd said when Liv demanded he stop teasing the new girl. Then, as if to prove himself unstoppable, the boy got even louder, yelling his hateful thoughts about the girl for all to hear.

As classmates gathered to stare, Liv felt the fear in the girl's eyes as a spreading burn in her own chest. Dropping her books, she pushed in between the bully and the girl, again ordering him to quit. The boy leaned down until he was nose to nose with Liv and with a smirk said again, 'Or what?"

It was a fair question. As the second-smallest girl in her grade with only pillow-fighting defense skills, Liv had no might and no plan. Still, she wasn't about to watch something so unkind and unfair play out in front of her. The meanness of it all was unbearable. Luckily, just as the bully started to shove, the janitor parted through the onlooking crowd and sent all involved to the principal's office. Like the last time she'd been found trying to pull free a boy dog piled by classmates, Liv would have to explain why she'd again been found in the middle of a battle that hadn't concerned her.

But it did concern her. Everything did. Life would be so much easier if she didn't feel everything all of the time. Instead, she was dragged along with other people's ups and downs like a tin can tied to a car bumper.

Finally, the principal came out of her office, escorting the only slightly humbled bully to the exit door.

Then it was Liv's turn. She followed the principal into the dreaded office, listening to the door click closed behind them. There they talked until the last bell of the day rang, and she was finally dismissed without punishment.

As Liv slung her backpack onto her shoulder and began walking home, the roar of a passing motorcycle made her jump. Its grating blast felt as though it'd been megaphoned directly into her flinching eardrums.

Loud feelings, loud noises...she had a theory that the volume knob on all of her senses must have gotten bumped to high as she'd entered the world. Bright lights triggered headaches; food textures were bumpy or slimy; clothes itched and pulled; and strong smells often hit her like a punch in the face.

If only her super-sensitivities were heroic superpowers, the benefits might outweigh the hassle of it all. Liv liked to imagine that in the movie world she'd be a mutant super hero named Hyper Feeler. Using her superhuman powers, she'd fight evil alongside other unlikely heroes. At least then being so hyper-aware would have a purpose. By the time she arrived home, Liv just wanted to get away from all people, feelings and noise. She retreated into the

sheet-tented fort in the corner of her room, and escaped into her iPad games for hours.

Making her bed the next morning, Liv imagined seeing the bully that day at school. A sense of doom suddenly came over her, like the feeling she had when storm clouds blew across the sun and left everything in sudden darkness and distorted shadows. Then, a fearful thought occurred to her. Though it had the same inner voice as all her other thoughts, it seemed different somehow, like an invisible troublemaker whispering in her ear. It said that for every wrinkle she left unsmoothed in her sheets, her brother would break that many bones. She knew it was a weird, superstitious thought like "step on a crack and break your mother's back." But somehow, this threatening thought demanded her attention as if it were a speeding car heading directly for her. So uncomfortable was she that, though her friends were waiting outside to walk to school, she spent an extra twenty minutes smoothing every last wrinkle from her sheets.

Just in case the worry-filled thought was some sort of predictive warning, she followed its directions. And the haunting feeling faded. But it wasn't long before another troublemaking thought appeared.

In the days to come, bossy thoughts pushed into her head more and more. If she didn't wash her hands five times, her whole family would catch a horrible disease. If she didn't blink to cancel out a bad thought before a person talking finished his sentence, a loved one would suffer. If she didn't follow each step of her morning routine the exact right way, she would have to start everything over again from the beginning or the day would be jinxed.

Liv knew the thoughts were crazy and so feared she might be too. But with the never-ending worry loop playing in her head, she kept doing the remedies of blinking, washing, and keeping her routine order, if only to buy a few moments of relief. By the end of the week, her hands were cracked and bleeding from the over-washing, she was blinking like she had a horrible eye tick, and it was taking her an extra hour to get ready for school in the morning.

Her friends noticed she was distracted and told her to lighten up, as if she knew how and just wasn't doing it. Liv was becoming more aware of how different her mind was from her friends. They worried about missing the school bus, but she was afraid someone would catch her cold and pass it to a weak grandparent who'd die because of her carelessness. While they chatted about who had a crush on whom, her thoughts were stuck circling around whether her family had picked the wrong religion and might be kept out of heaven.

It was exhausting. Liv longed for a holiday from her own head. She started having lunch in the library so her friends wouldn't see her blinking like a crazy person.

There she sat when Mr. Lane, the school counselor, walked through the library door. Dressed in his usual business suit and felt hat, he seemed to have walked straight out of a black and white photo from an old library book.

Kids liked Mr. Lane because he was kind, funny, and remembered everybody's name. He slowed to a stop at the table where Liv sat behind a propped-open book. Surprised to be noticed, she felt important and embarrassed all at once.

"Hello Miss Liv," he said.

"Hi," she said, too nervous to hold his gaze.

"You've been here by yourself a lot lately. Everything O.K.?" he said.

Liv meant to say she was fine. She wanted to say "no problem," but instead she burst into tears.

~ 9 ~

Quickly, she hid her face with her hands, but the tears wouldn't stop flowing. It was as if the floodgates had opened, and the pressure of all her worries could no longer be contained. Tears rolled down and around her fingers, falling in large drops onto her book.

"Right...There is my answer," Mr. Lane said with a nod. He pulled another chair to the table and gave her a supportive side hug. Taking a box of tissues from a nearby shelf, he placed it in front of her. "Could we maybe talk about what's going on?"

Liv took a tissue, blotted her eyes and nose, and tried to pull herself together. "If I tell you," she sniffed, "you might think I'm crazy...Maybe you'll think I should be locked up in a padded room."

"Well," said Mr. Lane. "I doubt it's as bad as all *that*." He leaned forward as if whispering a secret. "Besides, people who are *actually* crazy don't usually *know* they are."

Liv thought on this for a moment. She sniffed again, a little surprised the world hadn't come to an end when she'd spoken her fears out loud. Maybe she'd tell Mr. Lane a little more.

"It's just that I'm having a lot of weird thoughts, worst nightmare types of thoughts."

"Ok," said Mr. Lane, sitting up straighter. "So we're dealing with intrusive thoughts."

Liv looked at him, surprised. "That's... like, a thing?"

"Sure. Everybody has them now and again," he said.

Liv's shoulders relaxed a little. "The thing is it's not just sometimes. They won't leave me alone. And some of the thoughts are just *awful*!" She shook her head in disgust and lowered her voice so that no one else would hear. "Like I might see myself, clear as a movie in my mind, shoving someone I love down a hill. But, I would *never* do that, *never ever!*" She looked at him, desperate for him to understand. "But these ugly thoughts are in my head. So they must represent the kind of person I am."

"Really?" said Mr. Lane with a calm smile, "because it seems to me that you are shocked and upset by such thoughts. Doesn't that make who you are the opposite of those thoughts?" Liv thought about this, hoping he was right. "If," Mr. Lane continued, "you had to buy all your thoughts from a salesman, would you buy those thoughts?"

~ 13 ~

She looked at him horrified, "I'd pay to have them taken away!"

Mr. Lane nodded, knowingly. "Right, so these thoughts are not wanted. Surely, you've had a song stuck in your head before, right?"

Liv nodded that she had.

"I mean one you really hated?"

Liv smiled, "Usually."

"Did you write that song?"

She laughed a little, "No."

"Does it belong to you? Does it represent your beliefs?"

Liv thought of one particularly silly song that always got stuck in her head, "For sure not!"

Mr. Lane lifted his eyebrows, "Right? And why is that? Because thoughts are just pieces of ideas that blow into our minds like fall leaves on a breeze. They are *suggestions* that can be accepted or rejected, argued or ignored. Any number of ideas can wander into our thought space triggered by movies, books, websites, daydreams, fears, overheard conversations, other people's judgments, etc."

"A thought is like an email that shows up in your mind's inbox. Some are useful, others are junk. Sometimes the junk mail even tries to disguise itself as the important kind, hoping to get you to open and respond to it. That a thought appears in your inbox is not the problem. The trouble comes when you decide it's worthy of opening, assign meaning to its contents, and respond to it with self-judgment and panic."

"Why can't I just think like a normal person? I have so many thoughts that come with a second thought riding piggyback to judge the first one. Was it a good thought or a bad thought? Am I good or bad for having it?"

Mr. Lane smiled. "You must feel like you're living two lives at once, one as the experiencer and the other as the observing judge."

Liv looked at him with surprise. "Exactly!" she smiled briefly before growing serious again. "But lately my thoughts seem meaner, almost bullying. They say that if I don't do some stupid thing, like blink three times, I will be to blame for something horrible happening."

Mr. Lane's expression surprisingly spread into a smile. "You must be a Sensitive," he said, as if he'd just told her great news. "Sensitives tend to be beautiful people who sometimes have to deal with these kinds of unwanted thoughts. In our inner worlds, these bullying thoughts are known as Thought Crows."

Liv's facial expression must have appeared as puzzled as she felt because Mr. Lane repositioned himself and tried to explain in a different way.

"There is this outer world where we interact with each other in our physical shells, doing our everyday tasks. But within each of us is the force of who we are."

"That force has been called by many names: soul, self, spirit, mind, etc. And that self is the rightful ruler over our own inner world, our Kingdom of Mind."

Mr. Lane felt around in his coat pocket and pulled out a pair of wire-rimmed eyeglasses.

"May I show you what I mean?" he said, holding the eyeglasses open and ready to wear in front of her face. Liv nodded, a little unsure of his plan. As he placed them onto her nose, she could not have been more surprised.

Through these extraordinary glasses she could see amazing structures sitting atop her classmates' heads like magical crowns.

She couldn't help but stare at a girl casually pulling a book from a library shelf, seemingly unaware that she wore a palace upon her head, complete with towering columns and spires.

Mr. Lane continued, "Just as a microscope lets you

see into the tiny cellular world unseen to the naked eye, so these specs will give you a peek into the inner world of our Kingdoms of Minds."

Liv pointed through the library window at two boys reading on the grass outside. "His looks like some kind of courthouse or maybe a school." She squinted to better see every detail.

"Oh!" she said with great excitement. "Is that a stadium on the head of the second boy?"

Mr. Lane nodded that it was. "Maybe the first will become a lawyer or a teacher. The second might decide to be an athlete. Each Kingdom of Mind is as unique as our fingerprints, built on an individual mix of talent and potential."

"Incredible," Liv murmured to herself. Then it occurred to her that she would also have a kingdom to see. With great excitement, she said, "I need a mirror to see my own!"

"There's an easier way," said Mr. Lane. Taking the glasses from her nose, he tucked them back into his coat pocket. Then, with both hands, he lifted his felt hat from his head and placed it onto hers, holding it there for what seemed a long minute.

"That should do it," he said, turning it over. From within the rim of his hat rose a brilliantly-colored castle with wide-open courtyards and sloping green hills. Stirring from somewhere within her came a joy she hadn't felt in what seemed a very long time.

"It's exactly the kind of kingdom I would have wanted," she said with awe.

Mr. Lane chuckled, "That's because it's yours. It's you." He peered more closely over the contents of

his hat. "And it is just as I guessed," he smiled. "You have the kingdom of a Sensitive, complete with its identifying red 'S' flag."

"Some of my favorite people are Sensitives," he said. "They tend to be kind, intelligent people who care about others and expect a lot from themselves." He pointed to her castle, "Just look how many windows you have to let in the light of kindness and the warmth of compassion."

"Look there," he pointed to the lands around the castle, "green fields of imagination and trees filled with the fruits of creativity. Many of the world's greatest poets, artists, musicians, and leaders have just this kind of a Kingdom of Mind." He winked, "It's a powerful one."

Then, something seemed to catch Mr. Lane's eye, and he leaned in for a closer look. "I think I see the source of your problem." He pointed to a tree filled with black dots. "There are the Thought Crows I told you about," he said. Liv looked to see that the dots were in fact crows: loud, cawing, clicking, scolding crows.

"What exactly do they want?" Liv asked.

"The energy of your attention," said Mr. Lane.

"That's it?" She asked.

"Well," Mr. Lane raised an eyebrow. "That can grow to be a lot. You see, for a thought, attention is food. Most thoughts don't ask for much of it. They might remind you of a joke or to brush your teeth, that kind of thing. But Thought Crows play dirty. They will take the shell of a thought and fill it with fear, hoping to catch your focus and get you to throw them the seeds of your attention."

"Everything you don't want to be, they will accuse you of being. Every event you would hate most to happen, they will threaten will come true if you don't follow their instructions."

Here, Liv thought, were the invisible troublemakers that had been chattering in her ear. She felt sick to her stomach as a thought occurred to her.

"Does that mean that because I've been feeding these nightmare thoughts my attention they will get strong enough to come true?"

"Heavens no," said Mr. Lane, "Thought Crows have

no such power. All they can do is grow stress and negativity inside your Kingdom of Mind. And by getting you to focus on fear, your attention is taken away from people who love and need you, from all that you might create, and from the joy that rightly belongs to you."

"Who knows," Mr. Lane winked, "you might even end up in the library at lunch."

She laughed a little under her breath.

"Shall we look back in time to see when the Thought Crows first arrived?" Mr. Lane asked.

"We can do that?" Liv asked.

"You can do as you like. It's your kingdom. Just use this," he said, handing her the eraser-side of a pencil, "to push on the front door knocker for entry."

Peering into her kingdom there inside Mr. Lane's hat, Liv found the tiny front door and pressed the eraser to the lion head knocker.

Her castle collapsed flat before transforming into a slim screen that rose again from the hat. On it, she could see a street-view image of her Kingdom of Mind.

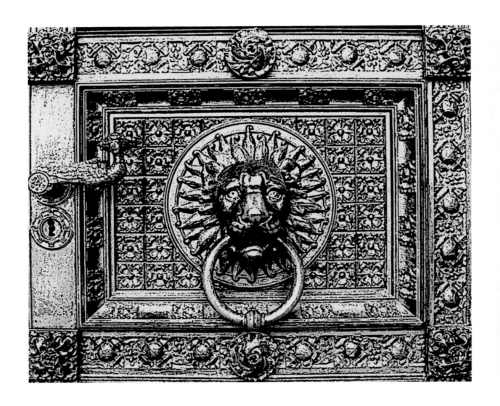

"Swipe your finger from left to right to rewind your
view back through time," Mr. Lane said. Liv did so,
amazed as she panned passed the incredible details
of her kingdom. There were beautiful, tall buildings
with ornate balconies and hand-painted flower boxes
that overflowed with color.

Mr. Lane marveled, "Look what can be built with the
tools of creativity!" Black metal poles protruded
from the castle walls holding decorative metal signs
with her best ideas painted in elegant gold lettering.

"It is too quiet in this part of your Kingdom of Mind," Mr. Lane said. "Your energy must be being spent elsewhere, likely in the fields with the Thought Crows."

As Mr. Lane spoke, their view of cobblestone streets turned to that of rolling, bright green fields. So rich were the colors of her kingdom that those in the outer world paled in comparison.

Before today, Liv would have expected her mind to have been a cob-webbed, shadowed place. Never would she have imagined it to be so full of magic and rich inner resources.

As she scrolled their view closer to the Thought Crow filled trees, the noise from the birds' scolding caws was incredible.

"It's no wonder I can't hear my other thoughts!" Liv said over the racket.

On the screen she saw an image of herself face to face with a single Thought Crow. Its shiny black head cocked sideways, seeming to focus on a sack tucked into her screen self's belt.

"It's staring at that sack," she said.

"In it are the seeds of your attention," said Mr. Lane.

Liv looked closer and noticed that mixed into the crow's glossy chest feathers was the word FEAR. She suddenly had that sense again that bad things were coming, like when scary movie music gets louder right before something terrible happens onscreen. Just then, Liv's screen image placed her hand over her stomach.

"What's happening there?" Mr. Lane asked, pointing to the screen.

"Stomach cramps," she said. "It happens when I start to worry."

"Mmmhmm," said Mr. Lane. "Thought Crows know how to ride in on the winds of worry like birds in the outer world know how to glide in on a breeze."

"See how your shoulders are hunched up by your ears?" Mr. Lane pointed at the screen. "You're tensing your muscles. These are your body's worry signals. Take note of them."

The sound of the FEAR Crow's caw twisted into words she could understand. "Bad things are

BAD THINGS C... ...EJECTION MEANNESS PAIN
PEOPLE GE... ...OUSES BURNING BETRAYAL
VIRUSES A... ...URRICANES TORNADOES
EARTHQU... ...ER PAIN HOSPITALS THIEVES
SICKNESS... ...RT ANGER ENEMIES BULLIES
TEASING... ...ING TEASING DISOWNING
CAR HIT A... ...SNAKE BITES SPIDERS
PLANE CR... ...BY LIGHTNING BITES
POISON... ...ING DOG ATTACKS
ALLIGATO... ...OUNDS GASHES
BAD THIN... ...EANNESS PAIN
PEOPLE GE... ...IG BETRAYAL
VIRUSES AC... ...ADOES
EARTHQUAKE... ...THIEVES
SICKNESS DEA... ...ULLIES
TEASING HATIN... ...WNING
CAR HIT AND RUN... ...IDERS
PLANE CRASHES FIR... ...NG BITES
POISON BLOOD CHOK... ...ATTACKS
ALLIGATORS PRISON ST... ...ASHES
BAD THINGS COMIN... ...REJECT... ...S PAIN
... ...RAYAL
EARTHQUAKES...
SICKNESS DEATH HURT ANGER ENEM...
TEASING HATING STABBING TEASING D... ...ING
CAR HIT AND RUN KIDNAP SNAKE BITES ...RS
PLANE CRASHES FIRE STRUCK BY LIGHTNI... ...TES
POISON BLOOD CHOKING FALLING DOG A... ...KS
ALLIGATORS PRISON STEALING WOUNDS GASHE...

~ 29 ~

coming for people you love unless you do what I say."

As Liv's screen self started arguing with the FEAR crow, she watched as it took the sack from its belt and began feeding the creature the seeds of her attention.

"Wait…" Liv said, pointing at the screen.

"What am I doing?"

"You are taking what the FEAR Crow said seriously. And as you argue your defense, you are feeding it the energy of your attention," Mr. Lane said, watching the scene.

"But I don't want to give it anything!" she said.

"The FEAR crow shrieked out "Disease! Fire! Contamination!"

Another Thought Crow swooped down from a nearby branch. In its feathers Liv read the words WHAT IF.

"When one Thought Crow gets fed, others are quick to follow," said Mr. Lane. He pointed at the squawking WHAT IF bird.

WHAT IF BAD THINGS FEAR WHAT IF HURT
FEAR WHAT IF RE JECTED FEAR WHAT IF
DISEASE WHAT IF LOVED ONE DIES FEAR
WHAT IF HIT BY CAR FEAR WHAT IF I'M NOT
ENOUGH FEAR WHAT IF TORNADOS, FEAR
WHAT IF FLOODS WHAT IF FIRE WHAT IF
FIGHTING FEAR WHAT IF DIVORCE FEAR
WHAT IF SPIDERS WHAT IF POISONED FEAR
FEAR WHAT IF CHOKED WHAT IF PLANE
CRASHED FEAR WHAT IF STABBED FEAR
WHAT IF KIDNAPPE_ ___ IF ABUSED
FEAR WHAT IF CA_ ___ON
WHAT IF STRUCK ___AT IF
ACCIDENT F___BBED FEAR
WHAT IF TH___ AT IF HOUSE
BURNED DOW___STERS WHAT
IF UNLOVED ___OTTEN FEAR
WHAT IF ALON___ DOG BITES
WHAT IF CO___AR WHAT IF
HURT SOM___WHAT IF HELL
WHAT IF BA___HURT PEOPLE
FEAR WHAT IF___BRINGS BAD
LUCK FEAR WHA___EAR WHAT IF
TOO FAT WHAT ___NY FEAR
___T IF LAUGHE___HAT IF
W___WHAT IF L_SE C___FEAR
W___ON_HAT IF SNAKES WHAT IF
BR___NG WHAT IF THIEVES
WHAT___FEAR WHAT IF
DROWN___N FEAR
WHAT IF B___RGET
WHAT IF LOS___
FEAR WHAT IF I

"This one's goal is to make you believe that something highly unlikely, like getting poisoned by a spider that only lives in Africa, could happen as easily as something very probable, like the school bell ringing for your next class."

The WHAT IF crow's rattle turned into words "What if you get stung by a scorpion? What if poison gets slipped into your drink? What if someone wasn't wearing a seatbelt and fell out of the car because you didn't close the door properly?"

Liv's screen self covered her mouth in horror before throwing the WHAT IF crow more seeds of her attention.

"Even though," said Mr. Lane, "Sensitives may be quite certain that the WHAT IF crow's story has no basis in truth, their powerful imaginations are able to picture the narrative's every awful detail. This makes the horror stories *feel* more possible than they actually are."

"Sensitives have a way of seeing constant possibilities and often are desperately looking for reassurances that the negative ones will never happen. But you have to retrain yourself to live with the uncertainty of not being able to control everything. Ground yourself in the reality of the probable, meaning the more likely of possibilities, because you only have a certain amount of energy to spend. You can't waste it on every imagined possibility."

Liv watched her screen self duck suddenly under the enormous wingspan of another crow swooping down over her head. As it swung its claws forward like a plane lowering its landing gear, she read the word DOUBT in its feathers. Once touching ground, the Thought Crow lowered its head and let out a long, grating call.

"You might not have locked the door," DOUBT said, cocking its head as it stared expectantly at the bag of attention seeds in her hand. "You've forgotten before. You'd better check."

Another crow hopped closer to her image on the screen. It had BLAME written in its feathers.

Mr. Lane murmured, "Where there is DOUBT there is usually BLAME."

"You're so careless," BLAME called out. "You want a thief to rob your brother because you were angry with him yesterday," it screeched.

MAYBE I FORGOT I COULD BE WRONG I'M NOT SURE MAYBE NOT
FORGET I DON'T KNOW A LOT OF THINGS IT'S HAPPENED BEFO[R]
MAYBE I HURT H[IS] FEELINGS I COULD HAVE [BEEN] WRONG DOUB'
GERMS CAN S[?] PROBABLY GOT IT WRO[NG] [DID]NT CLOSE I[T]
MIGHT H[AVE] [U]NDONE I DIDN'T [DO] [IT] WELL ENOU[GH]
MAYBE I [?] LONG ENOUGH [?]K NOT SU[RE]
MESSE[D] [WO]RK HARD ENOU[GH] [M]Y FAULT
[A]LL BE[?] [I'M] ALWAYS LATE [?] ENOUGH
DON'T U[?] THINGS AS WELL A[?] DO MESS
[I]F I WASN'T SO SEL[F]ISH IF WASN'T SO LAZY [?]RELESS
CAUSED IT I SHOULD HAVE KNOWN MY FAUL[T] IF [I] [WAS] FASTE[R]
THEY ALWAYS SAID I COULDN'T MY FAULT I'M RESPONSIBLE AGA[IN]
SPACED OUT AGAIN [I'M] NOT STRONG ENOUGH OR F[I]T ENOUGH [?]
MAKE BAD CHOICES I'M SLOW MY FAULT I'M RE[SPO]NSIBLE AGAIN
[I]F I WAS A BETTER PERSON I KNOW BETTER MY FAULT MY FAUL[T]

DOUBT BLAME

Then it followed with, "Horrible thoughts belong to horrible people!"

Mr. Lane held his hands up in a time-out position. "Here's where these fowl have fouled in their logic," he smiled. "Like the best liars, Thought Crows build their false stories upon the smallest grain of truth. In this case, maybe you had a moment of passing anger towards a family member, completely normal. Knowing you can't deny that bit," Mr. Lane continued, "the Thought Crow will use that tiny pebble of truth as the foundation for a ridiculous, guilt story."

BLAME cawed, "You're a bad person. You're selfish…You're not smart enough." Liv cringed and watched as her screen self threw attention seeds by the handfuls while it argued with BLAME.

Mr. Lane shook his head, looking at her with understanding.

"Not one positive word from this lot. There never is from Thought Crows."

Just then a sleek crow squawked loudly from the stump of a nearby tree. "I wondered when that one would get here," said Mr. Lane. "FAKE FIXER usually follows once the others have laid the groundwork for him. His job is to offer a fake solution to the fear story the other Thought Crows have set in motion."

FAKE FIXER Crow rattled a series of remedies. "Tap on the sides of the door when you walk into a room in order to cancel the bad thought you just had," it said.

"It sounds ridiculous when I hear it out loud," Liv

said, shifting uncomfortably. "You know, I don't even think these bullying thoughts in whole sentences anymore. All I need is the trigger idea to remind me of the whole fear story, and I just start doing the remedy for relief."

"It works better for the Thought Crows if you don't think too much about what they are saying and whether it makes any sense," said Mr. Lane.

"They do their best work in the unthinking undercover. If they can train you into the habit of responding to a trigger without examination, then they have a kind of automated energy payment plan with you: trigger, response, and repeat."

"That's why it's so important to bring the patterns of thought and illogical responses into the light of your conscious mind. Write down the scripts of their fear stories on paper so that you can see and identify them for what they truly are."

"The Thought Crows would prefer you stay stuck in the hamster-wheel of their negative thought loops, though. Maybe then you won't remember that *you* are actually the ruler of this entire Kingdom of Mind and the only one in it who truly has any power."

Liv thought about this. "That's right," she said. "I have a kingdom! I must have an army of soldiers. I'll order them to wage war on the Thought Crows!"

Mr. Lane shook his head, "You can't kill a thought. It's just mental energy that will shift form."

Liv's hopeful posture slouched in discouragement.

"Then how will I ever fight them?"

"If you want to defeat them, you don't fight." Mr. Lane smiled.

"Seriously?" Liv said in frustrated disbelief.

"You have been fighting them with counter thought all this time. How's that been working?"

Liv thought how much worse everything had been getting, even though she was trying so hard to think and do everything right.

"What if," Mr. Lane said, lifting one finger to the air, "instead of arguing and wrestling with every fear story presented, you just let them exist? You see, your participation is required for the Thought Crow's game to work. If you don't respond, they won't survive without the food of your attention."

"But I've tried to ignore them before," Liv said. "And things just got worse."

"Well sure, at first hungry Thought Crows used to eating well will squawk louder when kept from being fed. But just keep choosing not to engage with them. Retraining your mind in new habits of response takes practice as you learn to live with

the discomfort of not answering. Thankfully, being perfect is not necessary. Sensitives have a way of thinking that whatever they do has to be faultless. Just doing *better* is the goal. And for every fear thought you resist answering, you are already better than before."

"Should you catch yourself feeding the Thought Crows, just recognize it and pull the plug on the thought conversation. Even though you feel uncomfortable, turn your thoughts elsewhere. As you keep at it, the Thought Crows will eventually, one by one, fly away, restoring peace to your Kingdom of Mind."

"So, they'll leave and never come back?" Liv said, hopefully.

"Oh no, they'll try to come back," Mr. Lane said matter-of-factly. "Who wouldn't want to live in a Sensitive's beautiful kingdom, feeding from such high quality attention?"

"But just keep refusing to feed them. And remember," he said, pulling a coin from his pocket. "Every coin has two sides. A Sensitive has this side," he pointed to the back side of the coin, which

represents the thin boundaries between your
sensitive self and the world. It requires that you set
up measures to protect your good, open nature. But
then you also have this other side to your coin," he

said smiling. And with the same fingers that were holding the coin, he swiveled its face forward.

"And this beautiful side is absolutely needed by this world. It's the side that knows what suffering looks like, and that is able to perceive emotional dimension in people and situations that others may not notice at all."

"This is the side where your sensitivity gives you insights for counseling, teaching, art, and more. It allows you to use your compassion in thoughtful acts to make the lives of people around you better every day. Just like the person who is born with the voice to sing incredibly, as a Sensitive, you are born with the heart and awareness that can comfort and serve the world. You are built the way you are for a reason."

Liv thought on that. Maybe there was a use and benefit for her hypersensitive powers after all. She rubbed her face with her hands, "Sometimes I just think, why me?"

"Well, just you and thousands of Sensitives around the world," said Mr. Lane.

"They really have the same kind of mind I do?" Liv asked.

Mr. Lane raised one eyebrow, and with a half-smile, nodded that they did. "Likely, even people in your own family tree have faced similar struggles, as the condition of Thought Crows is often an inherited challenge."

"And not just people from all different time periods, countries, and cultures have had problems with Thought Crows, but also some of the kids walking the school hallways with you every day."

"But how come I never see them?" Liv said, looking up at Mr. Lane.

He chuckled, "Do they ever see you?"

Liv remembered how hard she had worked to hide her remedies.

"So big is the problem," Mr. Lane continued, "that the outer world even has a name for the condition of Thought Crows: Obsessive Compulsive Disorder or OCD for short."

"The O is the FEAR/WHAT IF story the Crow tells. The C is the action FAKE FIXER tells you will solve the problem the other Thought Crows presented. And the D just stands for disorder, meaning it is a known problem."

"Though there are many types of Thought Crows specializing in a vast variety of fear stories, they are just branches of the same tree of OCD."

The two of them looked at the screen. The video playback had moved forward in time to show the swirling dark mass of Thought Crows that was currently roosting in her Kingdom of Mind.

"But there are so many of them and only one me."

Mr. Lane chuckled, "They have played their part well if the ruler of the kingdom thinks these pests have such power. You **ARE** the power. And just as you are not alone as a Sensitive in the outer world, you are not on your own in the inner one either."

"What do you mean?" Liv asked.

"As the ruler of your Kingdom of Mind, you have a Council of Inner Advisors at your disposal," he smiled.

"Let me show you," he said.

He directed her to push the home button on the screen. As she did, the image changed from crow-filled trees to a grassy hill on which stood the silhouettes of five people.

Mr. Lane called out, "General Awareness, can you hear me?"

A wise-looking gentleman in a military uniform stepped forward. Standing very upright, he

saluted and said in a steady voice, "At your service."

Mr. Lane looked at Liv, "Remember when we talked about you feeling like you lived the life of an observer and an experiencer all at once?" said Mr. Lane.

Liv nodded that she did.

"Well, General Awareness will show you how to use your natural observational powers as a Sensitive to work to your advantage. He will help you identify which thoughts come from Thought Crows and which are just your average variety of thought."

The general added, "I will teach you to become conscious of your thought patterns. And just like farmers in the outer world set up nets and shiny objects to keep out pests and protect their harvest, so also can you learn to keep Thought Crows from feeding on the seeds of your attention."

"That's right," said Mr. Lane. "Furthermore, General Awareness will teach you how to notice your body's response to worry. Remember how worry makes your stomach cramp?"

Liv nodded.

Mr. Lane continued, "Since the condition of having Thought Crows or OCD is considered to be an anxiety or worry disorder, it is important to become aware of the process of worry as it appears in your body."

"Exactly," said General Awareness. "When your mind senses danger, it puts the body into the state known as 'Fight or Flight mode.' It's your body's kind of emergency response system to help you fight off or run from danger, like an attacking bear."

"But people with anxiety and OCD have a way of over-triggering their bodies' emergency systems. Thought Crows take advantage of your mind and body's state of panic to better sell the their stories, since in the midst of so much upset, FEAR, DOUBT, BLAME, AND WHAT IF stories *feel* entirely believable."

Mr. Lane asked General Awareness, "What signs should Liv look for that show her body might be moving into panic mode?"

General Awareness, dutifully answered, "Shallow and fast breaths, a pounding heart, sweating, shaking, and tight muscles are some Fight or Flight signs."

"I feel the pounding heart and tight muscles a lot," Liv admitted.

General Awareness nodded. "Once you learn to notice your body's stress responses, I'll show you how to reverse the panic process by breathing like a relaxed person."

Liv crinkled her eyebrows, "But how can I breathe calmly when I'm all freaked out?"

General Awareness smiled. "Square breathing, it's one of my favorite tricks."

"Is it hard?" Liv asked.

"Not at all," the general smiled. "But like everything, practice helps you get better. Now, you know how in games, like Hide and Go Seek, children count 'one-one thousand, two-one-thousand' to make sure they keep a steady counting pace?"

Liv nodded that she did.

"Well, that's the speed at which you should count in your head for Square Breathing."

"Like a square with four sides, there are four steps. For the first step, represented by the first side of the square, breathe a steady breath in while counting one-one-thousand, two-one-thousand, three-one-thousand, and four-one thousand."

"For the second step or side of the square, hold the breath for the same count of four. You let out the breath to the count of four for the third side of the square. And finally, for the fourth side, you hold your breath again for the same count of four."

"Repeating this pattern of well-paced breathing can help stop your body's panic process, putting you in a much stronger position to confront the challenges the Thought Crows present."

"Thank you General Awareness," Mr. Lane said, with a slight bow of his head. The general smiled, saluted, and stepped back in line.

"Now," said Mr. Lane, "once the general helps you become aware of a Thought Crow's presence, all intelligence gets passed to Major Disengage."

A bearded soldier with a blank expression stepped forward and saluted. "Yes Ma'am," said the serious Major Disengage. "My job is to help you unplug all communication from bullying thoughts."

"No matter what the Thought Crow says, I will not authorize response: no canceling, arguing or debating…just dead air," he said, jutting out his jaw

and standing proudly.

"May I ask a question?" said Liv, leaning closer into the screen to make sure the major could hear her.

"Certainly, Ma'am," said the major.

"If I unplug from my thoughts, aren't I going to be sort of blank?"

"No, Ma'am. It's just important that you learn to be in the presence of FEAR's thoughts without obeying FAKE FIXER's solves. Once you can live with the discomfort of not responding to the Thought Crows, then you intentionally can plug your attention into more positive thoughts.

Mr. Lane added, "So, let's say your thoughts tell you to repeatedly wash your hands beyond the basic level or horrible things will happen. You, with the help of General Awareness, will recognize and label the thought as coming from the Thought Crow FEAR. Knowing this, you don't rewash your hands in response, even when it feels so hard not to do so. Once you have resisted the urge to listen to FAKE FIXER, you can plug your thoughts into doing something more enjoyable, like a sport, hobby or game. Of course, if you're in the middle of school, a conversation or homework, just pick up and place your focus back on the subject in progress."

"Exactly," said the major.

Mr. Lane saluted Major Disengage and turned back to Liv. "General Awareness and Major Disengage are your first line of defense. As you break the habit of doing FAKE FIXER's silly remedies, you will come to see that the doom they promised does not occur.

The more you persist and prove to yourself the emptiness of the Crow's threats, the easier it will become to ignore them."

Mr. Lane smiled as he looked back to the Council on the hill. "Ah, there is no more essential member of your council than the next in line for introduction. Here is Higher Self."

A noble-looking woman stepped forward in the likeness of Liv's imagined version of herself as a grown up. She wore a calm, reassured smile, and Liv trusted her immediately.

Mr. Lane continued. "She is the keeper of your inner knowing and holder of your truth. When the scam artists FEAR, WHAT IF, BLAME, and DOUBT Thought Crows fill your head with lies, look within to Higher Self. She knows exactly who you truly are, what you mean and value, and what you would never do. When you move passed the noise of worry and consult her, she will provide you the wisdom of her quiet, inner knowing. Trust her goodness."

With her chin held high with confidence, Higher Self winked at Liv.

"Once General Awareness, Major Disengage and Higher Self have helped put you back in balance, you have two other members of your Council ready to help you strengthen your Kingdom of Mind."

Mr. Lane waved forward a studious man with round glasses whose arms were filled with books, papers and a laptop. "Here is Noble Knowledge."

"Hello there," the studious man nodded, his hands too full to wave. "I would love to help empower you with information."

"By reading and learning about the condition of Thought Crows under its outer world name: Obsessive Compulsive Disorder (OCD), you'll know how to better understand this challenge you face as a Sensitive. There are many articles, books, and association websites that have written about this condition."

"With the guidance of a trusted adult or librarian, you can find information on OCD tailored to your age and reading level," said Noble Knowledge with a smile. "I can also help you learn about different OCD medications to talk with your doctor about. Sometimes they can help make the Thought Crows not seem quite so loud."

"I am ready to learn," Liv smiled. Noble Knowledge returned a broad smile.

"The final member of your Council, though young, is of invaluable importance." Mr. Lane signaled a smiling girl forward. The sweet girl carried a fluffy bundle in her arms. Liv cooed with delight seeing it was actually two fluffy, small dogs.

"Here is Jester Joy," said Mr. Lane. "Her happiness and the delight she brings will help lift your energy out of the lows of negativity."

"There is so much fun to have," Joy said with a pure smile of delight. "I will remind you of what makes you happy, like playing with animals, dancing to happy music, watching funny movies, going out with friends, and playing games with loved ones."

Mr. Lane nodded, "Joy keeps you focused on all that is good in life. Instead of seeing only the negatives in your day, she will help you start to notice the positives. Together, you might even make lists of things that you are grateful for so that you will start to notice even more things to be happy about."

Joy continued, "I'll also help you put things on your calendar to look forward to in the midst of the work of retraining your mind."

Mr. Lane added, "Joy's playfulness and bouncy optimism have a way of scaring off Thought Crows."

"I'm so glad to meet you," Liv smiled.

"I can't wait to play together," Joy beamed.

Liv turned to Mr. Lane "This Royal Council is with me at all times?" she said, amazed.

"Always has been. Always will be," said Mr. Lane.

"Grant them the power and they will help you restore order to your Kingdom of Mind."

Liv smiled and leaning closer over the hat said, "I intend to keep you all close." The Council beamed smiles in return.

Just then the bell rang, making Liv jump and bringing her back to the reality that she was still at school. Lunch was over, and she only had five minutes to get to class.

Mr. Lane looked at her knowingly. They took a moment to say their goodbyes to all the Council members on the hill who did the same with much well wishing. Mr. Lane directed Liv to press the lion door knocker icon that was in the far right-hand corner of the screen.

As she did so, the screen lowered and repeatedly folded itself until it disappeared back into Mr. Lane's hat. He then placed it back on his head, gave it a pat, and, inhaling a deep breath, stood to his feet.

Smiling at Liv, he said, "Will you stop by my office from time to time and let me know how things are going?"

"Yes…for sure," Liv said, also standing. Feeling so grateful, she couldn't help but rush forward to give Mr. Lane a hug. He laughed and hugged her back. Then, tucking in his library chair, he turned and walked towards the library exit.

As Liv quickly jammed the book she'd been ignoring back into her backpack, she looked after Mr. Lane. As he passed through the doorframe of the library exit, he turned and lifted his hat in a goodbye gesture. There, atop his head, within a ring of clouds, Liv saw an amazing castle that reminded her of her own. Sure enough, flying over the structures of his kingdom, there waved the red flag of a Sensitive. She smiled broadly and laughed out loud.

From deep within she heard Higher Self say, "Everything's going to be O.K."

And, for the first time, in a very long time…she knew it was true.

The End...And the Beginning

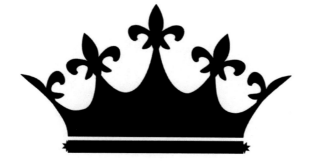

ABOUT THE AUTHOR

Having struggled with OCD as a young child, S.K. Clark writes with deep compassion for sensitive children facing the same challenge. As a freelance writer and former magazine editor, S.K. has a Bachelor of Arts in Communication and is a regular contributor to OCD support groups.

Website: skclark@kofmind.com

https://www.facebook.com/KingdomofMind

Made in the USA
Las Vegas, NV
22 January 2021